Easy Christmas Recipes: The Best Christmas Holiday Cookbook

OLIVIA NELSON

INTRODUCTION

There's nothing I enjoy more than having my family gathered around in the kitchen and cooking for Christmas dinner. It's one of the only days of the year when we can put aside all of the things that tie us down during everyday life, come together as a family and enjoy each other's company without any major distractions.

Planning for a Christmas party or even your Christmas dinner menu can be tedious and time-consuming. I have done the hard work for you and put together this cookbook with 100 recipes that will knock your socks off. These recipes are so good that you'll be making them year-round, even when there isn't something to celebrate!

Happy Holidays!

Olivia

Appetizers

Antipasto Skewers

Ingredients:

12 small balls of fresh mozzarella (jarred in oil, if possible)

12 kalamata olives

12 green olives, pimento stuffed

12 slices of salami, cut thick

12 small pepperoncini peppers

6 whole jarred cherry peppers, halved

1 dozen 7-inch skewers

Preparation:

Thread one of each ingredient item onto the 7-inch skewers.

Serve right away. Store the rest, covered, in the fridge for up to 24 hours.

Smoked Mozzarella Cheese Dip

Ingredients:

1 cup provolone cheese, shredded

1 cup smoked mozzarella cheese, shredded

½ cup parmesan cheese, grated

1 cup sour cream

pinch of red pepper flakes

1 teaspoon Italian seasoning

1 tablespoon fresh parsley, chopped

1 roma tomato, seeded & diced

1 baguette loaf, sliced

Preparation:

Preheat oven to 450 degrees.

In large bowl, mix together parmesan cheese, provolone cheese, mozzarella cheese, sour cream, red pepper flakes and Italian seasoning.

Grease a 1½-quart casserole dish with nonstick cooking spray. Pour the sour cream mixture into the dish.

Bake in the preheated oven for about 15 minutes or until the mixture is melted and bubbly. If you like a browned top, broil for 2-3 minutes more (being careful not to burn). Garnish with chopped parsley and diced tomatoes.

Bake bread slices for about 5 minutes and then serve right away.

Cheeseball Bites

Ingredients:

1 (8 ounce) container Kaukauna spreadable cheese (Smoky Cheddar flavor)

8 ounces of cream cheese

2 teaspoons pimento, chopped

2 tablespoons butter

1 tablespoon green pepper, finely chopped

1 teaspoon Worcestershire sauce

1 tablespoon onion, finely chopped

1½ cups bacon bits

½ teaspoon lemon juice

1½ cups chopped walnuts

Preparation:

In a bowl, combine margarine, cream cheese, and cheese spread. Microwave for about 25 seconds to soften. Mix well.

Stir in Worcestershire sauce, onion, green pepper, pimento, and lemon juice. Chill in the fridge for about 30 minutes.

Roll the mixture into 1-inch balls, and then roll half of balls in walnuts and the other half in bacon bits. Place pretzel stick in each ball and serve immediately, or refrigerate until served.

Serve with extra pretzel sticks or crackers!

Bacon Wrapped Chicken with Cream Cheese

Ingredients:

4 boneless skinless chicken breasts

12 slices bacon

8 ounces of cream cheese, softened

1 tablespoon chives, chopped

Preparation:

Preheat your oven to 375 degrees.

Add bacon to a large frying pan set over medium heat and partially cook bacon (should still be flimsy). Drain bacon on paper towels.

Mix together chives and cream cheese in small bowl and set aside.

Place the chicken breasts in plastic bag and flatten with a meat mallet (or hit with rolling pin) to about ¼-inch thickness.

Spread a spoonful of cream cheese mixture in the center of the chicken, leaving a ½-inch gap from edges.

Start with the smallest end of the chicken breast and roll to wrap up the cream cheese mixture.

With the seam side facing up, wrap cooked bacon pieces around chicken, keeping it wrapped. You can secure the wraps with toothpicks.

Place the wrapped chicken in a baking dish and bake for about 30 minutes. Turn the oven to broil for about 5 minutes or until bacon is crisp. Sprinkle with more chopped chives, if desired, and serve immediately.

Hasselback Chicken with Spinach & Goat Cheese

Ingredients:

4 boneless skinless chicken breasts

3 cups fresh spinach

½ teaspoon crushed red pepper flakes

½ cup crumbled goat cheese

2 teaspoons paprika

⅓ cup mozzarella cheese, shredded

salt and pepper

Preparation:

Preheat your oven to 350 degrees. Line a baking sheet with foil and set aside.

Add a splash of olive oil to a large skillet. Sauté spinach over medium heat for about 3-5 minutes or until slightly wilted. Stir in crumbled goat cheese and cook for about 1 minute or until cheese is melted.

Stir in red pepper flakes, and set aside.

Arrange the chicken breasts in the baking sheet and with a sharp knife, cut the chicken into slits, about ¾ of the way through the breasts and about ½-¾ inch apart.

Stuff each chicken slit with spinach mixture and generously sprinkle with salt and pepper; season with paprika and sprinkle with ¼ of mozzarella cheese over each breast.

Bake for about 20-25 minutes. For more browned and bubbly cheese, turn your oven to broil for the last 10 minutes of cooking.

Pumpkin Pie Dip

Ingredients:

2 cups whipped topping

2 cups powdered sugar

12 ounces of cream cheese

1 cup canned pumpkin

1 teaspoon pumpkin pie spice

1 teaspoon ground ginger

graham crackers

Preparation:

In a bowl, beat together powdered sugar and cream cheese until light and fluffy.

Stir in spices and pumpkin.

Fold in whipped topping and refrigerate for at least 30 minutes before serving.

Serve with graham crackers.

Italian Sausage Stuffed Mushrooms

Ingredients:

24 ounces of white button mushrooms

⅓ pound ground hot Italian sausage

8 ounces of cream cheese

6 cloves garlic, minced

½ yellow onion, finely diced

3 teaspoons fresh thyme leaves, chopped

⅓ cup dry white wine (such as Sauvignon Blanc)

¾ cup parmesan cheese, grated

1 egg yolk

salt and pepper

Preparation:

Using a damp paper towel, wipe off the mushrooms. Use a paring knife to remove stems of mushrooms and finely chop the stems. Set aside.

Cook the sausage and crumble finely; transfer to a plate and let cool.

Lower heat to medium low and stir in garlic and onion. Sauté for about 3 minutes.

Stir in wine to deglaze, scraping with a wooden spoon to release browned sausage bits. Cook until most of the liquid is evaporated.
Stir in chopped mushroom stems along with thyme. Sauté for about 2 minutes. Stir in salt and pepper and transfer the mixture to a plate to cool.

In a bowl, mix together parmesan cheese, egg yolk, and cream cheese. Stir until well combined. Stir in sausage and onion mixture and cover with plastic wrap. Refrigerate for about 30 minutes or until firm.

Preheat your oven to 350 degrees. Line baking sheet with parchment paper. Transfer the mushroom mixture into the mushroom cavities, pressing to fill. Bake for about 25 minutes or until golden brown. For a more golden brown topping, broil the last minute.

Let cool a bit and sprinkle with chopped parsley to serve.

Hot Ham & Cheese Rollups

Ingredients:

1 pound of ham, thinly sliced

1 can refrigerated crescent dough

12 slices Swiss cheese, thinly sliced

1 tablespoon dried minced onion

1 tablespoon poppy seeds

½ cup butter, melted

1½ tablespoons yellow mustard

½ teaspoon Worcestershire sauce

Preparation:

Preheat your oven to 350 degrees. Coat a 9×13-inch baking dish with non-stick spray.

Roll out dough and press into a 13×18-inch rectangle; top with cheese and ham.

Starting with the long side, roll dough up tightly, pinching the end together. Place the rolled dough, seam-side down on a surface; cut into 12 equal pieces.

Arrange the rollups, evenly spaced, in the baking dish.

In the meantime, combine onion, poppy seeds, butter, and Worcestershire sauce in a small bowl. Pour evenly over the rollups and bake, uncovered, for about 25 minutes or until lightly browned.

Loaded Devil Eggs

Ingredients:

6 slices bacon, cooked and chopped

12 large eggs, hard-boiled, cooled and halved

2 teaspoons fresh chives

2 tablespoons Dijon mustard

2½ teaspoons white vinegar

2 tablespoons sharp cheddar cheese, finely grated

¼ teaspoon garlic powder

¼ cup + 1 tablespoon sour cream

salt and pepper

paprika

Preparation:

Scoop the egg yolks out of the hard-boiled egg halves and place in a bowl.

Stir in bacon, garlic powder, mustard, vinegar, chives, cheese, mustard, salt and pepper.

Stir in sour cream and spoon the mixture back into the egg halves until filled. Sprinkle with paprika.

Refrigerate until served.

Spinach & Artichoke Dip Stuffed Mushrooms

Ingredients:

1 pound whole white mushrooms

1 cup spinach, wilted

1 cup canned or jarred artichoke hearts, chopped

2 ounces of cream cheese, softened

⅓ cup parmesan cheese, grated

⅓ cup mayonnaise

1 teaspoon garlic, minced

¼ teaspoon Italian seasoning

salt and pepper

Topping Ingredients:

¼ cup breadcrumbs

3 tablespoons parmesan cheese, grated

½ teaspoon Italian seasoning

Preparation:

Preheat your oven to 400 degrees. Grease a baking dish and set aside.

Cut stems from the mushrooms and set aside.

In a bowl, mix together parmesan cheese, cream cheese, Greek yogurt (or mayo), spinach, Italian seasoning and garlic. Stir in artichoke hearts, salt and pepper.

Scoop out spoonfuls of spinach mixture and press into each mushroom until filled. Arrange the stuffed mushrooms into the baking dish.

In a bowl, stir together the remaining parmesan cheese, breadcrumbs, and Italian seasoning. Sprinkle the mixture over the stuffed mushrooms and cover the dish with foil.

Bake for about 15-20 minutes. Uncover and continue baking for 5 minutes more or until mushrooms are tender and the top lightly browned. Serve warm.

Spinach & Artichoke Dip Garlic Bread

Ingredients:

1 loaf baguette

1½ cups mozzarella cheese, shredded

14 ounces canned artichoke hearts, drained and chopped

10 ounces of baby spinach leaves

8 ounces of cream cheese

3 cloves garlic, minced

3 green onions, sliced

3 tablespoons butter

parmesan cheese, grated

½ tablespoon oil

salt and pepper

fresh basil leaves or Italian parsley, chopped

Preparation:

Preheat oven to 350 degrees.

Cut baguette into four equal pieces. With a knife, remove the inside of the loaf, leaving some bread around the edges. Set aside.

In a large pot set over medium high heat, heat oil until hot. Stir in artichoke and cook for about 1 minute.

Lower the heat to medium and stir in spinach. Cook until wilted.

Stir in mozzarella and cream cheese. Cook until cheese is melted. Stir in green onions, salt and pepper. Remove the pan from heat and set aside.

Using a wooden spoon, stuff baguette quarters with spinach mixture. Place the stuffed bread on a cutting board, lining them up to fit together as they did before bread was cut. Slice into 1-inch thick slices.

Cut a piece of heavy duty foil that is approximately 6-inches longer than the bread. Slide the bread slices off the board and onto the foil, keeping them together.

In a bowl, combine garlic and butter. Cover and microwave for about 1 minute or until butter is melted. Brush the garlic butter mixture over the bread, making sure all the garlic gets on top of the bread.

Fold the foil around the bread and bake for about 15 minutes.

Unwrap foil and continue baking for 5 minutes more or until lightly browned. Remove from oven and sprinkle with parmesan cheese and parsley leaves or basil. Serve warm.

Sweet & Spicy Sausage

Ingredients:

32 ounces smoked sausage, cut into ½ inch pieces

12 ounces of grape jelly

12 ounces of chili sauce

1 teaspoon extra-virgin olive oil

½ teaspoon cayenne pepper

½ tablespoon garlic, minced

½ tablespoon crushed red pepper

Preparation:

Add oil to a small pan set over medium heat. Stir in garlic and sauté for about 30 seconds. Mix in grape jelly and chili sauce. Cook for about 10 minutes, stirring constantly.

Place sausage in a slow cooker. Stir the spices into the sauce mixture and then pour over the sausage. Cook, covered, for about 1½-2 hours on high or until the sauce is bubbly.

Stir once through cooking.

Million Dollar Dip

Ingredients:

1 cup cheddar cheese, shredded

1½ cups mayonnaise

5 green onions, chopped

½ cup almonds, slivered

½ cup cooked bacon, chopped

Preparation:

In a small bowl, combine bacon bits, mayonnaise, cheddar cheese, green onions, and slivered almonds.

Mix until well blended and refrigerate for at least 2 hours.

Serve with crackers.

Deep Fried Olives

Ingredients:

1 (10 ounce) jar garlic stuffed olives, drained

¾ cup Italian seasoned breadcrumbs

olive oil

1 egg, beaten

Preparation:

In a small bowl, beat the egg. Add the olives and stir to coat well.

Add breadcrumbs to a shallow dish. Place the egg-soaked olives on a plate and coat well with the breadcrumbs.

Fill a saucepan 2 inches deep with olive oil. Heat over medium-high heat until hot.

Working in three batches, fry the olives in the heated oil for about 45 seconds or until golden brown. Drain the olives on a paper towel and serve warm.

Bourbon Whiskey Meatballs

Ingredients:

1 pound frozen meatballs

½ cup brown sugar, tightly packed

½ cup ketchup

¼ cup bourbon whiskey

1 teaspoon Worcestershire sauce

1 teaspoon fresh lemon juice

Preparation:

In a bowl, combine all ingredients (except meatballs) and mix well.

Place meatballs into a crock pot and add whiskey sauce. Stir until the meatballs are well coated with the sauce.

Turn the heat to high and cook, stirring occasionally, for about 1 hour or until the meatballs have thawed.

Reduce the heat to low and let simmer for 10 minutes.

Brie & Cranberry Bites

Ingredients:

14 ounces of puff pastry sheets

6 ounces Brie

6 tablespoons cranberry sauce

1 egg, whisked

Garnish: fresh thyme leaves

Preparation:

Preheat your oven to 400 degrees. Line a baking tray with parchment paper.

Unroll the puff pastry and generously brush with egg wash. Cut into 40 rectangles.

Arrange one rectangle on top of the other and repeat until you have 20 doubled rectangles of pastry.

Arrange them on the baking tray and bake for about 10 minutes. Remove from oven.

Slice Brie into small pieces and arrange them over the pastry puffs. Return back to oven and bake for 1-2 minutes more or until brie is melted. Serve puffs on a platter and top each with a dollop of cranberry sauce and fresh thyme leaves.

Parmesan Crusted Crab Cake Bites

Ingredients:

8 ounces of cream cheese, softened

6 ounces of fresh lump crabmeat, drained

⅔ cup parmesan cheese, grated & divided

1¼ cup panko breadcrumbs

1 teaspoon Dijon mustard

3 tablespoons mayonnaise

1 teaspoon Worcestershire sauce

½ teaspoon lemon zest

1 egg yolk

¼ cup butter, melted

¾ teaspoon Old Bay seasoning

1½ tablespoons fresh parsley, chopped

Garnish: chive aioli

Preparation:

Preheat your oven to 350 degrees. Grease two, 12-cup standard muffin pans.

Remove any bits of shell from the crabmeat.

In a large bowl, stir cream cheese until very smooth. Add ⅓ cup of parmesan along with the next 6 ingredients and whisk until smooth. With your hands, fold in parsley and crabmeat.

In medium bowl, combine melted butter, breadcrumbs, and the remaining parmesan cheese. Toss with a fork until the breadcrumbs are moistened.

Spoon about a tablespoon of the bread mixture into each muffin cup, pressing into the bottom and up the sides to make the crust.

Spoon about a tablespoon of the crabmeat mixture into each crust and bake for about 25 minutes or until golden brown.

Remove from oven and let cool for about 5 minutes in pans. To loosen, run a knife around the edges of the crab cakes and gently lift the cakes from the pan. Serve topped with chive aioli.

Cranberry & Pecan Mini Goat Cheese Balls

Ingredients:

16 ounces of cream cheese, softened

4 ounces of white cheddar cheese, grated

4 ounces of goat cheese

½ cup pecans, finely chopped

½ cup dried cranberries, chopped

¼ cup chives, thinly sliced

Coating Ingredients:

30 pretzel sticks

½ cup pecans, finely chopped

½ cup chives, thinly sliced

½ cup dried cranberries, chopped

Preparation:

In large bowl, combine all ingredients and stir until well blended. With a spoon, scoop out small balls and roll them with hands.

Add cranberries, pecans, and chives into separate shallow bowls. Roll cheese balls into the coating and then spear with pretzel stick.

Chill in the fridge until ready to serve.

If you're preparing at least 4 hours in advance, do not use pretzel sticks until ready to serve. Serve the cheese balls with assorted crackers and pretzels.

Hot Crab Dip

Ingredients:

1 pound shelled lump crab meat

8 ounces of cream cheese, softened

⅓ cup sour cream

⅓ cup mayonnaise

2 tablespoons shallots, minced

2 tablespoons fresh lemon juice

2 teaspoons extra-virgin olive oil

½ teaspoon hot sauce

⅓ cup parmesan cheese, grated

2 tablespoons chives, minced

¼ teaspoon salt

1 tablespoon dill, minced

⅓ cup parmesan cheese, grated

Preparation:

Preheat your oven to 425 degrees. Grease an ovenproof baking dish with butter and set aside.

Heat olive oil in a small pan over medium-high heat. Add shallot and sauté for about 3 minutes or until tender and lightly browned. Remove the pan from heat and let cool.

In a bowl, beat together sautéed shallots, chives, ⅓ cup parmesan cheese, sour cream, mayonnaise, cream cheese, hot sauce, lemon juice, salt and dill until well blended and creamy.

With your hands, fold in the crabmeat and spread the mixture evenly into the baking dish. Sprinkle with remaining parmesan cheese and bake for about 20-30 minutes or until bubbly and lightly brown on top.

Garnish with dill and chives. Serve with crackers or toasted baguette slices and lemon wedges.

Drinks

Pineapple Cranberry Punch

Ingredients:

1 (2 liter) bottle of ginger ale

juice from 2 limes

4 cups pineapple juice

4 cups cranberry juice

1 cup coconut rum

1 cup silver rum

Preparation:

In a pitcher, combine lime juice, coconut rum, silver, pineapple, and cranberry juice.

Add fresh cranberries and lime slices.

Serve in a glass and top with ginger ale. Enjoy!

Cranberry Mojito

Ingredients:

1 cup sugar

1 cup fresh cranberries

1 cup water

For each serving:

2 ounces of rum

10 mint leaves

2 ounces of cranberry simple syrup

1 tablespoon lime juice

seltzer water

Preparation:

Combine water, cranberries and sugar in a medium sauce pot. Simmer over medium heat for about 10 minutes, or until the mixture turns pink. Remove from heat and cool to room temperature.

In a tall glass, combine lime juice and mint leaves. With a fork, slightly muddle to release the mint flavor.

Fill the glass with 2 ounces of rum, 2 ounces of cranberry syrup and ice. Top with seltzer water and garnish with cranberries.

Champagne Punch

Ingredients:

1 bottle champagne, chilled

2 cups cranberry juice

1 cup water

3 cinnamon sticks

½ cup sugar

¾ cup pineapple juice

4 whole cloves

1 lemon, quartered

red rimming sugar

Preparation:

In a small pot, mix water, cloves, cinnamon sticks and sugar. Bring to a gentle boil and lower heat. Simmer for about 5 minutes.

Meanwhile, rim the champagne glasses with lemon and dip the rim into the red sugar.

Remove the pot from heat and discard cloves and cinnamon

sticks. Cool completely and then pour into a large pitcher.

Add pineapple juice and cranberry juice. Chill until ready to serve.

To serve, add chilled champagne and serve in the rimmed glasses.

Cranberry Orange Punch

Ingredients:

3 cups cranberry juice

2 cups club soda

2 cups apple cider

⅓ cup agave nectar

⅓ cup orange juice concentrate, thawed

1 cup cranberries

1 cup crushed ice

7 cinnamon sticks

7 orange wedges

1 apple, thinly sliced

Preparation:

In a pitcher, mix orange juice concentrate, apple cider, cranberry juice, and agave in a bowl. Place orange wedges over cinnamon sticks.

Add a few apple slices and cranberries to a serving glass with about ¾ cup of juice mixture and a little ice.

Fill each glass with club soda and garnish each with cinnamon stick.

Holiday Sangria

Ingredients:

2 bottles Pinot Grigio

1 Granny Smith apple, chopped

¼ cup sugar

¾ cup sparkling apple cider

¾ cup cranberries, whole

¼ cup cranberries, halved

3 rosemary sprigs

Preparation:

In a large pitcher, stir together all ingredients until sugar is dissolved.

Refrigerate for about 4 hours or until chilled and serve.

Christmas Punch

Ingredients:

1 (2 liter) bottle 7-Up or Sprite

12 ounces of vodka

1 (12 ounce) can of frozen limeade concentrate

1 (12 ounce) can of frozen orange juice concentrate

4 cups cranberry juice cocktail

ice cubes

Garnish: cranberries

Preparation:

In large bowl, combine all ingredients until well mixed.

Serve garnished with cranberries.

Christmas Cosmopolitan

Ingredients:

16 ounces of triple sec

8 ounces of vodka

1 (64 ounce) bottle of white cranberry-peach juice

1 (64 ounce) bottle of cranberry juice

lime juice

corn syrup

coconut flakes

Preparation:

Mix all ingredients together in a large pitcher. Chill for at least 4 hours.

Shake with ice and strain into a glass rimmed with lime juice, corn syrup, and coconut flakes.

Nutella Hot Cocoa

Ingredients:

4 cups milk

2 tablespoons unsweetened cocoa powder

2 tablespoons Nutella

2 tablespoons sugar

Garnishes: crushed hazelnuts, chocolate chips or Nutella

Preparation:

In a medium saucepan set over medium-high heat, heat milk until warmed through.

Whisk in sugar, cocoa powder, and the Nutella spread until dissolved and well blended.

Bring the mixture to a gentle simmer, stirring frequently.

Remove from heat and serve with favorite garnishes.

Jolly Jingle Juice

Ingredients:

1 (750ml) bottle Whipped Vodka

1 (2 liter) bottle Cherry 7-Up

1 bottle Pink Champagne or Sparkling Rosé

Garnish: cranberries

Preparation:

Chill vodka, 7-Up and champagne in fridge for at least 4 hours.

In a large pitcher or a punch bowl filled with ice, stir together all ingredients until well mixed.

Serve over ice and garnish with cranberries.

Gin & Appletiser

For 1 serving:

1 cup Appletiser original, chilled

¼ cup of gin, chilled

slice of apple

cinnamon stick

wedge of lime

3 cranberry ice cubes

Ingredients for Ice Cubes:

filtered water

frozen cranberries

ice cube trays

Preparation:

Take your empty ice cube trays and add four cranberries to each compartment. Top with water and freeze overnight or until firm and no cranberries float.

Serve Appletiser and gin in a glass and add apple slice, cinnamon stick, and 3 ice cubes. Squeeze in lime juice and

enjoy!

Christmas Sangria

Ingredients:

1 bottle of dry red wine (such as Cabernet Sauvignon)

¼ cup Grand Marnier

¼ cup agave nectar

¼ cup brandy

¾ cup ginger ale

½ cup pomegranate seeds

1 lime, sliced

1 orange, sliced

1 pear, sliced

2 sticks of cinnamon

Preparation:

In a large pitcher, combine brandy, Grand Marnier, agave nectar, pomegranate seeds, pear, lime, orange, and cinnamon stick. Stir until well combined.

Add bottle of red wine to the pitcher and refrigerate, covered, for about 2-3 hours.

When ready to serve, stir in ginger ale and serve over ice.

Jack Frost

Ingredients:

½ cup Blue Curacao

1 cup pineapple juice

½ cup cream of coconut (such as Coco Lopez)

½ cup vodka or light rum

2 tablespoon sugar

1 tablespoon water

3 cups ice cubes

Garnish: shredded coconut

Preparation:

Mix water and sugar in a small microwavable bowl. Microwave for about 1 minute, stir and continue microwaving for 1 more minute or until the mixture is thick, but able to be stirred.

Place shredded coconut on a plate and separate so there are no clumps. With a spatula, dab sugar mixture on the outside of glasses near the rim and then roll them in the coconut. Set aside.

In a blender, combine cream of coconut, blue curacao, vodka, pineapple juice and ice cubes. Blend for about 2-3 minutes or until smooth.

Pour the cocktail into the prepared glasses and serve right away!

White Christmas Punch

Ingredients:

1 (2 liter) bottle of 7-Up

½ gallon vanilla ice cream

½ cup sugar

¼ cup hot water

1 teaspoon almond extract

6 tablespoons evaporated milk

Garnishes: whipped cream and sprinkles

Preparation:

In small glass bowl, combine water and sugar. Microwave for about 30 seconds or until the sugar is dissolved. Let cool and then stir in almond extract and evaporated milk.

Pour the mixture into large punch bowl and stir in vanilla ice cream. Break the ice cream with a potato masher into small chunks.

Gradually stir in the 7-Up and spoon into glasses. Serve garnished with sprinkles and whipped cream, if desired.

Gingerbread Latte

Ingredients:

8 cups whole milk

3½ cups strongly brewed coffee or espresso

¼ cup pure maple syrup

3 teaspoons ground ginger

2 tablespoons brown sugar, packed

1 teaspoon vanilla extract

2 cinnamon sticks

½ teaspoon ground nutmeg

pinch of cloves

Garnishes: whipped cream, graham cracker crumbs, caramel sauce, and gingerbread cookies

Preparation:

Combine all ingredients in a slow cooker. Cook on low heat for about 3 hours or until heated through. Then cook on warm setting for about 2 hours, stirring occasionally.

Remove from heat and stir before serving.

Dip the rims of the serving cups into caramel sauce, and then into the graham crackers.

Serve the latte in the rimmed cups topped with caramel syrup and whipped cream, if desired. You can also top with gingerbread cookies!

Eggnog

Ingredients:

6 large egg yolks

2 cups milk

1 cup heavy cream

½ cup sugar

½ teaspoon nutmeg

¼ tsp vanilla extract

pinch of salt

Garnish: ground cinnamon

Preparation:

In medium bowl, whisk together egg yolks and sugar until creamy.

Combine milk, cream, nutmeg and salt in a saucepan set over medium high heat. Stir until it reaches a gentle simmer.

Slowly pour and quickly whisk a big spoonful of hot milk into egg mixture. Repeat until all the milk is used up. Return the mixture back to the pan and heat and whisk until the temperature reaches 160 degrees.

Remove the pan from heat and stir in vanilla.

Transfer the eggnog to a container and refrigerate, covered, with plastic wrap until chilled.

To serve, garnish with fresh whipped cream and cinnamon, if desired.

Kahlua Hot Chocolate

Ingredients:

2 cups milk

1 ounce Kahlua coffee liqueur

2 tablespoons sugar

¼ teaspoon cinnamon

1½ tablespoons unsweetened cocoa powder

pinch of nutmeg

Garnishes: mini marshmallows, salted caramel and chocolate syrup

Preparation:

Combine milk, nutmeg, cinnamon, cocoa powder and sugar in a medium saucepan. Heat the mixture over medium heat for about 2-3 minutes or until heated through.

Remove the pan from heat and stir in Kahlua.

Serve right away, garnished with chocolate syrup, salted caramel, and mini marshmallows, if desired.

Salted Caramel Eggnog

Ingredients:

¾ cup quality dark rum

5 eggs

3 cups whole milk

1 cup heavy whipping cream

¾ tablespoon pure vanilla extract

1 teaspoon grated nutmeg

½ cup caramel syrup

4 cinnamon sticks

⅔ cup white sugar

1 tablespoon sea salt

Garnishes: 2 egg whites, caramel syrup and sea salt

Preparation:

Combine cream, milk, vanilla, cinnamon, and nutmeg in a large saucepan. Bring to a gentle boil. Remove from heat and let sit for about 5-10 minutes to steep.

Beat eggs and sugar in a large bowl with stand mixer until fully blended. Pour the mixture into the milk mixture and whisk to mix well.

Mix in rum, sea salt and caramel. Whisk until well blended.

Beat egg whites in a bowl on high speed until foamy.

To serve, pour the eggnog into serving glass, leaving a small space on top. Top with egg whites and garnish with caramel sauce and nutmeg.

Enjoy!

Christmas Champagne

Ingredients:

1 bottle of quality champagne

pomegranate juice

pomegranate seeds

pomegranate syrup (½ simple syrup and ½ pomegranate juice)

green rimming sugar

Simple Syrup Ingredients:

Water

Sugar

Simple Syrup Preparation:

In a small saucepan, combine equal parts sugar and water over medium-high heat. Stir until dissolved.

Remove from heat. Allow syrup to cool. Refrigerate in an air-tight container until ready to use.

Preparation:

Make simple syrup by heating ½ cup of water, ½ cup of sugar, and pomegranate juice until the mixture starts to boil. Remove from heat and let cool.

Add green rimming sugar to a small plate. Slightly dip the rim of champagne flute into the syrup and then dip into the sugar, spinning the flute to cover the whole rim with sugar.

Add a tablespoon of pomegranate seeds into the flute and add 2 teaspoons of pomegranate syrup over the seeds.

Pour champagne to ½-inch below the sugar rim.

Enjoy!

Entrees

Cornish Game Hens

Ingredients:

2 (20 ounce) Cornish game hens

1 small green apple, sliced

¼ teaspoon pepper

½ teaspoon salt

Glaze Ingredients:

1 tablespoon Dijon mustard

2 tablespoons honey

1 tablespoon butter

¼ teaspoon curry powder

Preparation:

Preheat oven to 375 degrees.

Stuff the cavity of hens with apple slices and truss hen with string.

Rub with salt and pepper and arrange on a rack in a roasting pan. Roast for about 40 minutes.

In a small bowl, mix glaze ingredients together.

Remove hens from oven and brush with glaze. Continue roasting for about 20 minutes more, brushing occasionally with glaze as you roast until golden, and juices run clear.

Leg of Lamb

Ingredients:

1 (5-7 pound) lamb leg, bone-in

6 cloves garlic

3 tablespoons olive oil

3 stems fresh rosemary

coarse salt and freshly ground black pepper

Preparation:

Remove lamb from the fridge 1 hour before cooking.

Rub the lamb with olive oil and place it on a rack in a roasting pan. Drizzle with more olive oil and rub the oil into the meat. Sprinkle generously with salt and pepper.

Position the rack a few inches from the heat source and broil for about 5 minutes, or until the top is seared and browned.

Turn over the meat and continue broiling for 5 minutes more, or until the other side is seared too.

Remove lamb from oven and set oven to 325 degrees. Position rack in the center of oven.

Mince rosemary leaves and garlic and rub over the lamb.

Loosely cover the lamb with foil and return back to oven for about 1 hour or until the temperature of lamb reaches 135 degrees.

Remove lamb from oven and let rest for about 15 minutes before carving.

Place the lamb on a cutting board and cut to separate meat from bone. Cut into slices and serve.

Turkey Brine (for moist, flavorful turkey)

Ingredients:

2 gallons of cold water

3 cups apple juice or apple cider

2 cups brown sugar, packed

5 cloves garlic, minced

1½ cups kosher salt

4 tablespoons fresh rosemary

3 tablespoons peppercorns

peel of three large oranges

5 whole bay leaves

Preparation:

In large pot, combine all ingredients. Stir until sugar and salt dissolve. Bring the mixture to a gentle boil. Turn off the heat and cover.

Let the mixture cool completely and then transfer to a large pot or brining bag. Add the turkey into the brine and refrigerate for about 16-24 hours.

When ready to roast the turkey, remove from brine and place into a pot of fresh cold water. Let sit for about 15 minutes to reduce the saltiness.

Remove turkey from water and pat dry. Roast according to recipe for Perfect Roast Turkey.

Perfect Roast Turkey

Ingredients:

1 (14 pound) whole turkey, fresh or thawed

1 medium onion, peeled and quartered

1 teaspoon salt (omit if turkey has been brined)

1 teaspoon pepper

2 sprigs fresh parsley

2 sprigs fresh sage

2 sprigs fresh thyme

2 sprigs fresh rosemary

1 lemon, quartered

3 tablespoons olive oil or melted butter

Preparation:

Remove the turkey from the fridge and let rest for about 30 minutes.

Position the rack on the lowest position of the oven and preheat to 400 degrees.

Coat the rack and roasting pan with cooking spray and set aside.

Prepare the turkey: remove giblets and neck from the turkey and discard. Rub the turkey with salt and pepper, distributing inside the cavity and then stuff the cavity with herbs, lemon, and onion, reserving 1 onion quarter.

Overlap the skin at the cavity to try and cover as much gap as you can. Use small skewers or toothpicks to hold the skin. Use kitchen twine to tie the legs together.

Insert the remaining onion piece under the skin that covers the neck cavity. Tuck the wing ends under the body to hold the skin over the cavity in place.
Dry the turkey with paper towel and brush with olive oil until well coated. Place on a roasting pan, breast-side down.

To Cook the Turkey:

Place turkey in a 400 degree oven and cook, uncovered, for about 1 hour. Lower heat to 350 degrees and continue cooking for 1 additional hour.

Remove from oven and flip it over; insert a thermometer and return back to oven. Cook until the temperature reaches 165 degrees.

Remove from oven and check to make sure the thigh temperature is 165 degrees at the thickest part of the leg.

Cover with aluminum foil and let rest for at least 30 minutes. Carve and serve.

Garlic & Brown Sugar Pork Loin

Ingredients:

1 (2 pound) pork loin, trimmed of fat

2 pounds of potatoes, cubed

2 pounds of carrots, peeled and sliced

4 garlic cloves, minced

4 tablespoons brown sugar

¼ cup canola oil

1 tablespoon canola oil

salt and pepper

Preparation:

Preheat oven to 375 degrees.

In a bowl, mix together potatoes, carrots, ¼ cup canola oil, salt and pepper.

In a separate bowl, mix the remaining oil, garlic, and brown sugar. Rub mixture on the pork.

Line a large cookie sheet with foil and spread the potato mixture over it; make a space in the center of the veggies for the pork.

Add the pork and roast in oven for about 40-50 minutes or until the internal temperature is 150 degrees. Transfer the pork to a cutting board and let rest for about 5-10 minutes, covered with foil. Put veggies back in oven.

Remove the veggies from oven when ready to serve pork.

Roast Duck

Ingredients:

1 (6 pound) whole Pekin duck

1 lemon, chopped

5 garlic cloves, chopped

salt

Glaze Ingredients:

½ cup balsamic vinegar

¼ cup honey

juice of 1 lemon

Preparation:

If you're using a frozen duck, defrost it in the fridge for a few days before cooking.

When ready, remove the duck from the fridge 30 minutes before cooking to reduce chill.

Preheat oven to 350 degrees.

Prepare the duck:

Remove giblets from the duck and discard. Rinse duck with

cold water, both inside and outside. Pat dry and place it on a working surface.

With a knife, score the skin on the breast, being careful not to cut the meat, but only the skin. With the tip of the knife, poke all of the fatty parts of the bird to release fat.

Generously season the bird with salt, ensuring you season every part, including the inside cavity and the skin. Place the bird, breast side up on a roasting pan.

Stuff the duck cavity with lemon slices and five chopped garlic cloves and fold the flapping skin of the bird on both ends inwards to hold the lemon slices and garlic. Using kitchen twine, tie up the legs of the duck.

Roast the Duck:

Roast the duck in the roasting pan for about 1 hour at 350 degrees. Flip the bird over and continue roasting for 40 minutes more.

Remove the pan from oven and carefully transfer the bird to a large platter. Carefully pour the pan juices into a heat-proof bowl.

Return the duck back to the roasting pan, breast side up.

In a bowl, combine fresh juice of 1 lemon, and ½ cup balsamic vinegar. Brush the mixture over the duck and roast for another 40 minutes, brushing the bird every 10 minutes with the lemon mixture.

In another bowl, combine 3 tablespoons of the lemon-vinegar mixture with ¼ cup honey. Brush the breast side of the bird with the mixture and continue roasting for another 40 minutes, brushing every 10 minutes.

Remove the duck from oven and let rest for about 15 minutes.

Remove and discard the lemon from cavity and carve the duck.

Use pan juices to make a sauce or gravy, if desired.

Note: Duck should roast in oven for a total of 3 hours at 350 degrees.

Garlic & Herb Roasted Turkey

Ingredients:

1 (14 pound) whole turkey, fresh or thawed

¼ cup kosher salt

1 stick butter, softened

½ a yellow onion

cloves from one head of garlic, peeled

1 celery stalk, chopped into strips

1 tablespoon fresh sage, chopped

1 tablespoon fresh rosemary, removed from stem & chopped

1 tablespoon fresh thyme, removed from stem & chopped

zest of 1 lemon, plus the lemon

¼ cup olive oil

2 tablespoons black pepper

Preparation:

Remove turkey from the fridge and let it sit for about 30 minutes.

Preheat oven to 450 degrees.

In a medium bowl, stir together olive oil, lemon zest, softened butter, and herbs.

Season with salt and pepper.

Wash turkey under cold water and remove giblets and any gravy packets. Place it on a roasting pan and pat dry.

Generously rub the butter mixture all over the turkey, inside cavity, underneath and over the breast, wings, and under the skin.

Generously season the bird with salt and pepper and inside the cavity.

Stuff the halved lemon, garlic, celery and onion in the cavity and bake in oven for about 30 minutes.

Lower heat to 350 degrees, tent with foil and bake for 1½-2 hours or until the internal temperature reaches 165 degrees. Remove foil during the last 30 minutes of cooking.

Remove the bird from oven and let stand for at least 30 minutes before carving.

Garlic & Herb Beef Tenderloin with Horseradish Sauce

Ingredients:

1 (3 pound) beef tenderloin roast, trimmed and tied

2 teaspoons dried thyme

2 teaspoons dried oregano leaves

2 teaspoons dried crushed rosemary

2 teaspoons garlic powder

2 teaspoons coarse kosher salt

1 teaspoon dry mustard

½ teaspoon fresh ground black pepper

1 tablespoon olive oil

Horseradish Sauce Ingredients:

prepared horseradish (or freshly minced)

½ cup sour cream

3 tablespoons mayonnaise

dash of Worcestershire sauce

pinch of kosher salt

Preparation:

Prepare rub: in a small bowl, mix garlic powder, mustard, rosemary, thyme, oregano, 2 teaspoons of kosher salt and pepper.

Rub the roast with spice mix and wrap with plastic wrap. Refrigerate for at least 4 hours, for the meat to marinate.

Remove roast from the fridge and let sit for at least 1 hour before roasting.

Preheat oven to 450 degrees.

Unwrap the roast and place on rack in a roasting pan. Rub with olive oil and roast for about 15 minutes.

Lower heat to 325 degrees and continue roasting to your desired doneness.

Remove roast from the oven and tent with foil. Let sit for about 10-15 minutes before carving.

Meanwhile, prepare the Creamy Horseradish Sauce: combine all ingredients in a small bowl; served alongside the roast.

Garlic & Herb Pork Roast

Ingredients:

1 (5 pound) pork loin, trimmed & tied

10 small red potatoes

1 cup white wine

5 cloves of garlic

3 sprigs of rosemary

¼ cup of olive oil

pinch of red pepper flakes

salt and pepper

Preparation:

In a food processor or a blender, combine garlic, olive oil, white wine, rosemary, red chili flakes, and salt & pepper. Blend until smooth. Taste and adjust the seasoning, if desired.

pour the marinade over the pork roast and let marinate for at least 30 minutes.

Preheat oven to 400 degrees. Roast the pork for about 30-40 minutes or until the internal temperature reads 145 degrees. Remove the roast from oven and let rest for about 10-15 minutes.

Slice and serve.

Mustard Roasted Rack of Lamb

Ingredients:

1 (2 pound) rack of lamb

3 tablespoons Dijon mustard

2 tablespoons olive oil

1 tablespoon dried thyme

1 tablespoon dried tarragon

1 tablespoon dried marjoram

freshly ground black pepper

1 teaspoon kosher salt

Preparation:

Preheat your oven to 375 degrees.

In a bowl, mix marjoram, tarragon, and Dijon mustard. Set aside.

With a knife, score fat cap on lamb rack, making sure you do not cut into the meat. Season meat with salt and pepper.

In a heavy-bottomed pan, heat olive oil over medium high heat. Add lamb and sear on all sides for about 4-5 minutes on top and 1-2 minutes on bottom, or until light golden brown.

Generously brush the lamb with the mustard mixture and place on a roasting pan, bone-side down. Roast for about 20-25 minutes or until internal temperature reads 135 degrees.

Remove lamb from oven and cover with foil. Let rest for about 5 minutes and then slice.

Best Turkey Gravy

Ingredients:

2 cups turkey stock, (or turkey drippings, strained and oil removed)

6 cups water

2 smoked turkey wings

1 onion, coarsely chopped

4 ribs of celery, chopped

4 cloves of garlic, smashed

¼ cup all-purpose flour

½ cup whole milk

¼ cup unsalted butter

½ teaspoon kosher salt

1 teaspoon apple cider vinegar

Preparation:

Preheat oven to 375 degrees. In a large roasting pan, roast turkey wings, garlic, onion, and celery for about 2 hours.

Remove from oven. Add water to the pan and bring the mixture to a gentle boil. Lower heat and simmer for about 1 hour or until stock is reduced.

Strain stock into a large bowl. Refrigerate the liquid for at least 2 hours or overnight. Remove fat that is accumulated on top.

Melt unsalted butter in a large sauté pan. Whisk in flour and cook, whisking, over medium heat for about 2 minutes. Whisk in the turkey liquid and cook until the mixture is thickened.

Stir in apple cider vinegar, milk, and salt.

Red Wine Sauce (for beef)

Ingredients:

1¾ cups red wine

1¾ cups beef stock (or beef drippings)

⅓ cup balsamic vinegar

4 tablespoons olive oil

2 medium shallots, sliced thin

1 sprig rosemary

1 clove of garlic, lightly crushed

1 tablespoon of butter

Preparation:

In a medium saucepan, sauté shallots in oil over high heat, stirring, for 3 minutes or until lightly browned. Stir in garlic, rosemary, salt and pepper. Cook for 3 minutes more, stirring.

Stir in vinegar and continue cooking until liquid is reduced to one third.

Stir in stock and bring the mixture to a boil. Lower heat and simmer until liquid is reduced to one third again.

Discard rosemary and garlic and stir in a pinch of salt. Whisk in a knob of butter and add in any cooking juices from the steak or roast and serve.

Turkey Breast Roulade

You Will Need:

cheesecloth

kitchen twine

Ingredients:

3 cups of stuffing, uncooked

1 (3 pound) boneless turkey breast, butterflied

1½ tablespoon butter, melted

1 teaspoon salt

1 tablespoon olive oil

½ teaspoon black pepper

salt & pepper to taste

Sachet Ingredients:

½ celery rib with leaves, roughly chopped

¼ teaspoon whole black peppercorns

¼ yellow onion, roughly chopped

1 clove of garlic, smashed

2 sprigs of parsley

1 sprig of thyme

Gravy Ingredients:

4 cups reduced sodium chicken stock

½ cup white wine

2 tablespoons apple cider vinegar

1 tablespoon heavy cream

1 tablespoon + 1 teaspoon potato starch (or cornstarch)

salt and pepper to taste

Preparation:

Preheat oven to 325 degrees.

Place a rack in a roasting pan or on a sheet pan.

Place turkey between two pieces of plastic wrap on a work surface and pound it with a rolling pin or mallet to an even ¾-inch thickness.

Remove the turkey from the wrap and sprinkle with salt and pepper. Evenly spread the stuffing mixture over the turkey, leaving about a 3-inch border all round.

Place the remaining stuffing mixture into a greased baking dish and follow the instructions below.

Start with the shortest end of the turkey and roll up over the stuffing, tucking all stuffing inside. Tie firmly with kitchen twine every 2 inches to form a cylinder. Generously brush with butter and season with salt and pepper.

In a large roasting pan, Dutch oven or skillet, heat oil over medium high heat until hot, but not smoky. Add turkey, seam side down, and sear on all sides for about 5-6 minutes or until golden brown.

Place the turkey on the rack in the baking dish, reserving the gravy in the skillet for later use. Roast for about 1-1½ hours or until internal temperature reads 160 degrees.

Remove the roasted turkey from oven and transfer to a platter. Tent with foil and let rest for about 15 minutes before carving.

Meanwhile, make the gravy: lay a large piece of cheesecloth over a work surface and all ingredients in the center of the cloth; roll up the sides and tie with kitchen twine to form a sachet. Add the sachet and chicken stock to a saucepan over medium low heat. Bring to a simmer. Cook for about 25-30 minutes or until the stock is reduced to two cups. Set aside.

Set the pan in which turkey was seared in over medium heat. Add vinegar and wine and cook, scraping the bits on the bottom, until liquid is reduced by half. Stir in the stock and bring to a simmer.

In a bowl, mix 2 tablespoons and two teaspoons of water with potato starch. Whisk the starch mixture into the stock and simmer, stirring, for about 2-3 minutes or until the gravy is thick. Generously season with salt and pepper and reduce heat to low. Stir in heavy cream and continue cooking, covered, until ready to use.

To serve, strain gravy through a fine mesh sieve and adjust the seasoning.

Serve the turkey with gravy and the remaining stuffing.

Baked Ham with Brown Sugar & Pineapple Glaze

Ingredients:

1 (10 pound) bone-in fully cooked spiral-cut ham

½ cup brown sugar, packed

1 cup pineapple juice

4 cloves

1 cinnamon stick

Preparation:

Remove the ham from the fridge at least 2 hours before baking to reduce chill.

Remove the ham from the package. Rinse and dry with paper towels. Place the ham, fat side up, in a deep baking dish.

In a saucepan, combine pineapple juice, cloves, cinnamon stick, and brown sugar. Bring to a gentle boil. Lower heat to medium-low and simmer for about 15 minutes or until the liquid is reduced by half and it's thick and syrupy.

Brush the ham with half of the glaze, reserving the other half for later use.

Bake ham at 325 degrees for about 1¼ to 1½ hours. Remove from oven and brush with the remaining glaze. Continue baking for about 15-20 minutes or until the internal temperature reads 160 degrees.

Remove from oven and let rest for at least 15 minutes before serving.

Creamy Horseradish Sauce

Ingredients:

1 cup fresh horseradish, peeled & finely minced (or use prepared & drain well)

½ cup mayonnaise

½ cup sour cream

2 tablespoons fresh lemon juice

2 teaspoons Worcestershire sauce

1 teaspoon kosher salt

¼ teaspoon freshly ground black pepper

2-3 dashes Tabasco sauce

Preparation:

In a small bowl, mix all ingredients.

Refrigerate until served.

Apple Cider Glazed Turkey Breast

Ingredients:

1 (4-5 pound) turkey breast

2 cups spiced apple cider

1 medium onion

½ cup sage leaves, minced

6 cloves garlic

1 stick butter

1 tablespoon honey

4 teaspoons salt

1 teaspoon pepper

Gravy Ingredients:

2 tablespoons milk

¼ cup spiced apple cider or chicken stock

2 tablespoons flour

1 tablespoon apple cider vinegar

Preparation:

Preheat oven to 325 degrees.

Place turkey on a rack in a roasting pan, breast-side down.

Combine garlic, onion, pepper, sage, butter, and salt in a food processor. Blend until smooth.

With fingers, loosen skin from the bird and smear half of the butter mixture on the meat. Spread the remaining half on the skin and let sit, covered, overnight to marinate.

Combine honey and 1½ cups of spiced apple cider vinegar in a saucepan. Bring to a gentle boil and simmer until liquid is reduced to half a cup. Let cool to thicken.

Pour the remaining apple cider vinegar into the roasting pan and brush turkey with the spiced apple cider vinegar glaze.

Roast turkey in the pan for about 1½ to 2 hours, turning halfway through and basting with the glaze, until golden on the outside and the internal temperature reads 165 degrees. Remove from oven and let rest for 15-20 minutes.

Meanwhile, transfer the drippings to a saucepan set over medium heat. Whisk in flour until the paste comes together and separates from the excess fat. Pour out any excess fat and return the pan to the heat.

Whisk in milk and vinegar. Stir in apple cider vinegar until the gravy reaches desired consistency.

Slice the turkey and serve with gravy.

Best Ever Prime Rib

Ingredients:

1 (7 pound) bone-in prime rib roast

5 pounds of beef bones, including meat and fat

2 cups water

⅓ cup dry red wine

6 cloves of garlic, peeled and smashed

4 tablespoons olive oil, divided

3½ tablespoons kosher salt, divided

1 tablespoon + ½ teaspoon freshly ground black pepper

2 tablespoons Worcestershire sauce

½ teaspoon "gravy color" browning and seasoning sauce (such as Kitchen Bouquette or you can use liquid smoke)

Preparation:

Place roast on a plate and rub with oil, salt and pepper. Refrigerate overnight, fat side up and uncovered.

Preheat oven to 450 degrees, 5 hours before serving. Remove roast from fridge and let sit.

Meanwhile, place beef bones, beef fat, salt and pepper in a roasting pan. Roast for about 30 minutes. Flip the bones and fat and continue roasting for another 30 minutes.

Lower heat to 250 degrees and open the oven door to allow the oven temperature to come down.

Remove the roasting pan from oven and place garlic on top of the bones. Place roast on top of the garlic, fat-side up and roast until internal temperature reads 125 degrees.

Transfer roast to a plate and cover with foil. Let rest for about 20 minutes.

Raise oven temperature to 450 degrees.

Place the pan with bones over medium high heat and add wine to deglaze. Cook until wine has almost evaporated. Add gravy color (Kitchen Bouquette) and Worcestershire sauce. Simmer until the liquid is reduced to about 1 cup. Strain out the solids and return the juice to the pan.

Return the beef to the oven and roast for about 15-20 minutes or until browned and crisp.

Remove roast from oven and let sit for about 10 minutes before carving.

Heat the juice in the pan until hot and serve alongside the beef slices.

Sides

Croissant Mushroom Stuffing

Ingredients:

10 croissants, torn into bite-size pieces

12 ounces of cremini mushrooms, chopped

1 large onion, finely chopped

5 stalks of celery, finely chopped

3 large eggs, lightly beaten

½ cup fresh parsley leaves, chopped

1 tablespoon fresh thyme leaves, chopped

2 tablespoons olive oil

½ teaspoon sugar

Preparation:

Preheat oven to 350 degrees.

In a single layer, arrange the croissants on two rimmed baking sheets. Bake for about 10-20 minutes or until crisp and golden. Remove the croissants from oven and set the temperature of the oven to 400 degrees.

Coat a 2½-quart baking dish with non-stick spray.

In the meantime, heat oil in large saucepot over medium heat. Stir in onion, celery, thyme and ½ teaspoon of salt. Cook, stirring occasionally, for about 10-15 minutes or until almost tender.

Stir in the mushrooms and continue cooking, stirring occasionally, for 10 minutes more. Remove from heat.

Add eggs, sugar, parsley, croissants, and ½ teaspoon salt to the pot with veggies; fold until well blended.

Transfer the mixture to the prepared baking dish and bake, uncovered, for about 20 minutes. Uncover and continue baking for 10 minutes more or until crisp on the top and golden brown.

Twice Baked Sweet Potatoes

Ingredients:

4 large sweet potatoes

3 cups mini marshmallows

¼ cup brown sugar

¼ cup salted butter, melted

1 tablespoon sweetened condensed milk

1 tablespoon olive oil

1 teaspoon cinnamon

¼ teaspoon ginger

pinch of nutmeg

Preparation:

Preheat oven to 375 degrees.

Rinse the sweet potatoes and pat dry. Coat with olive oil. Using a fork, pierce the skin of the potatoes all over and place them on a baking sheet that is lined with parchment paper. Bake for about 70 minutes.

Remove from oven and let the potatoes cool for at least 10

minutes.

Cut the cooked potatoes into halves and scoop out the inside with an ice cream scoop or a spoon leaving about a ½-inch ring around the sides.

Place the scooped potato pulp into a large bowl. Return the emptied potato halves on the baking sheet.

Add ginger, sweetened condensed milk, melted butter, brown sugar, cinnamon and nutmeg to the bowl with the pulp and blend with a hand mixer until very smooth. Spoon the mixture back into the sweet potato halves, stuffing each slightly past full. Return to oven and cook for about 10-15 minutes. Remove from oven and set the oven to broil.

Stick marshmallows into the sweet potato halves until completely covered. Return to oven and broil for about 1-2 minutes or until marshmallows melt and begin to brown. Make sure the marshmallows don't burn.

Serve immediately.

Watergate Salad

Ingredients:

2 (8 ounce) cans crushed pineapple in juice, undrained

1 cup miniature marshmallows

1 tub frozen whipped topping, thawed

1 box pistachio instant pudding

½ cup toasted pecans, chopped

Preparation:

Stir together the pudding mix and full contents of pineapple cans. Mix well.

Fold in marshmallows and whipped topping. Refrigerate, covered, for at least 1 hour.

Top with pecans to serve.

Steakhouse Sweet Brown Bread

Ingredients:

2+ cups whole wheat flour

2 cups all-purpose flour

1 cup warm water

¼ cup honey

¼ cup brown sugar

1 egg

4 teaspoons active dry yeast

3 tablespoons molasses

2 tablespoons baking cocoa

2 tablespoons butter, softened

1 teaspoon salt

Preparation:

In a bowl with a stand mixer, combine yeast and warm water. Let yeast proof for about 10 minutes.

Stir in all ingredients, except whole-wheat flour. Beat until well blended.

Beat in 1 cup of flour and mix on low speed until blended. Gradually beat the remaining flour until dough comes together.

Transfer dough to a lightly floured surface and knead about 4-5 times, or until a tight ball forms. Cover and keep in a warm place for about 60 minutes, or until dough doubles in size.

Shape the dough into 16 equal-sized rolls and arrange them in a greased 9×13-inch pan. Let sit again for another hour. Bake in a 350 degree oven for about 22 minutes.

Roasted Brussel Sprouts & Butternut Squash

Ingredients:

3 cups brussel sprouts, ends trimmed, yellow leaves removed

1½ pounds butternut squash, peeled & seeded, cut into 1-inch cubes

3 tablespoons maple syrup

2 cups pecan halves

1 cup dried cranberries

5 tablespoons olive oil, divided

2-4 tablespoons maple syrup

½ teaspoon ground cinnamon

salt & pepper to taste

Preparation:

Preheat oven to 400 degrees.

Coat a foil-lined baking sheet with a tablespoon of olive oil and set aside.

Trim ends from the brussel sprouts and remove the yellow

leaves. Slice into halves.

Combine 2 tablespoons olive oil, brussel sprouts, and salt in a medium bowl. Toss until well coated and transfer to the prepared baking sheet, cut-side down. Roast for about 20-25 minutes, turning them once halfway through cooking.

Leave oven set to 400 degrees.

Coat a foil-lined baking sheet with a tablespoon of olive oil and set aside.

Combine 1 tablespoon of olive oil, diced butternut squash, cinnamon and maple syrup. Toss to coat well. Spread in a single layer over the prepared baking sheet and bake for about 20-25 minutes, turning once through cooking, until squash is tender.

Combine roasted butternut squash, roasted brussel sprouts, cranberries and pecans in a medium bowl. Mix well and serve.

Sweet Potato Casserole

Ingredients:

2 large sweet potatoes, baked until very tender (about 60 minutes at 350 degrees), peeled and mashed

2 tablespoons half and half

3 tablespoons butter

salt to taste

Pecan Topping Ingredients:

1 cup pecans, chopped

½ cup brown sugar, packed

⅓ cup butter

¼ cup flour

Preparation:

Preheat oven to 350 degrees.

In a bowl, mash the sweet potatoes, cream, butter, and salt. Transfer to a large dish or 3-4 ramekins.

In another bowl, mix butter, flour and sugar until crumbly. Fold in pecans and place the mixture on top of the potato mixture.

Bake for about 20 minutes or until bubbly and the top is lightly browned.

Serve right away!

Cranberry Sauce

Ingredients:

12 ounces of cranberries, fresh or frozen

1 cup sugar

1 cup water

Optional: orange zest, cinnamon, blueberries, raisins, currants, allspice, nutmeg

Preparation:

Rinse the cranberries in a colander, discarding any damaged or bruised cranberries.

In a medium saucepan, combine sugar and water. Bring to a gentle boil. Stir until sugar is dissolved. Add cranberries and return to a boil. Lower heat to a simmer and cook for about 10 minutes or until almost all cranberries have burst.

Leave the cranberry sauce as is or dress it up with your favorite ingredients. Try mixing in a few orange zest strips and ½ cup chopped pecans. You can also add in currants or raisins, or even the blueberries. Also holiday spices such as allspice, nutmeg or cinnamon are great additions.

Remove the sauce from heat and let cool completely. Transfer to a bowl and chill in the fridge.

Note: the sauce continues to thicken as it cools.

Creamed Corn with Bacon

Ingredients:

2 (12 ounce) packages frozen corn kernels

8 slices bacon, chopped

8 ounces of cream cheese, cubed

4 green onions, finely chopped

½ cup red onion, finely chopped

½ cup red bell pepper, finely chopped

2 tablespoons milk

1 teaspoon pepper

1 teaspoon sugar

½ teaspoon salt

Preparation:

In large skillet, cook bacon until crisp and brown. Transfer bacon to a paper towel lined plate and discard bacon grease, leaving a thin layer on the pan.

Add onion, red pepper and corn to the pan and cook over medium heat, stirring frequently, for about 6-8 minutes or until corn is heated through and veggies are tender.

Stir in milk and cream cheese until the cream cheese melts and the mixture is well blended. Stir in green onions, salt, sugar and pepper. Top with bacon and serve warm.

Garlic Mashed Potatoes

Ingredients:

10 Yukon gold potatoes, peeled and quartered

1⅓ cup milk

¼ cup sour cream

2 garlic cloves, smashed

3 tablespoons butter

1 tablespoon fresh chives, chopped

1 teaspoon salt

⅛ teaspoon ground pepper

Garnish: chopped chives

Preparation:

Add the potatoes to a pot with salted water and boil for 12 minutes, or until soft.

In a separate pot, boil 1⅓ cups of milk with 2 smashed garlic cloves. Remove from heat and let stand.

Drain the potatoes and mash them with the milk mixture, sour cream, butter, chives, pepper and salt until smooth.

Garnish with chives. Enjoy!

Classic Stuffing

Ingredients:

1 loaf day-old French bread, diced into 1/2-inch cubes and dried

2½ cups low-sodium chicken broth, divided

2 large eggs

2 medium yellow onions, finely diced

1½ cups celery, finely diced

⅔ cup Italian flat-leaf parsley, finely chopped

¼ cup fresh sage leaves, finely chopped

2 sticks unsalted butter, divided

3 tablespoons fresh rosemary (stems removed), finely chopped

2 tablespoons fresh thyme (stems removed), finely chopped

salt & pepper to taste

Preparation:

Preheat your oven to 250 degrees.

Arrange the bread cubes on a baking sheet and bake for 45 minutes, tossing occasionally, until completely dry.

Transfer the bread to a large bowl and set aside. Turn up the oven temperature to 350 degrees.

Grease a 9x13-inch baking dish and set aside.

Add 1½ sticks butter to a skillet over medium heat and sauté the celery and onions. Cook until soft, for 10 minutes and transfer to the bowl of cubed bread.

Mix in the herbs, 1¼ cups chicken broth, pepper and salt and toss well until evenly coated.

In a separate bowl, add the remaining broth and whisk with 2 eggs until well blended. Pour over the bread mixture and mix well.

Scoop into the baking dish and divide the remaining butter into small bits and sprinkle over the stuffing. Cover with foil and place in the oven to bake for 40 minutes.

Remove foil and continue baking for 40 more minutes until well browned.

Serve hot.

Twice Baked Potatoes

Ingredients:

6 russet potatoes

1 tablespoon kosher salt

2 tablespoons olive oil

Filling Ingredients:

1 cup sharp cheddar cheese

1 pound of bacon, cooked & chopped

1 bunch of green onions, chopped

6 tablespoons of butter

⅓ cup half and half

¼ cup sour cream

½ teaspoon kosher salt

¼ teaspoon of pepper

Preparation:

Preheat oven to 400 degrees.

Line a cookie sheet with foil and set aside.

Clean the potatoes and pat dry. Poke holes in potatoes using a fork. Rub olive oil on each potato and season with kosher salt. Bake for 1 hour.

Remove from oven and let the potatoes slightly cool. Scoop out the flesh of the potatoes into a bowl and mash with half and half, sour cream, butter, pepper and salt.

Use a spoon to scoop the potato mixture back into the skins and top with bacon, cheese and sliced green onions.

Bake for 10 minutes until the cheese melts.

Serve with sour cream.

Green Bean Casserole

Onion Topping Ingredients:

1 large onion

1 large egg

¾ cup panko breadcrumbs

½ cup all-purpose flour

1 tablespoon milk

½ teaspoon salt

¼ teaspoon ground black pepper

Casserole Ingredients:

1 pound fresh green beans, rinsed, trimmed and halved

8 ounces of mushrooms, quartered

1¼ cups half-and-half

¾ cup chicken broth

2 cloves garlic, minced

1 tablespoon + 1 teaspoon salt, divided

2 tablespoons unsalted butter

½ teaspoon ground black pepper

2 tablespoons all-purpose flour

Preparation:

Preheat the oven to 475 degrees.

Prepare a large baking sheet by lining it with parchment paper.

Add flour to a small bowl. In a second bowl, whisk the milk and egg together. In a third bowl, add the panko, pepper and salt.

Dip some thinly sliced onions in the flour, followed by the milk mixture and finally the panko mixture and arrange them on the baking sheet. Repeat this with the remaining slices. Bake for 25 minutes, turning them twice.

Remove from oven and reduce the temperature to 400 degrees.

Blanch the beans in a gallon of salted boiling water for 5 minutes and drain. Transfer to a bowl of ice water to retain their green color. Drain well, then set aside.

Melt butter in a large skillet over medium heat and sauté the mushrooms. Season with pepper and salt and cook for 5 minutes, until soft.

Stir in the garlic and cook for 2 minutes. Sprinkle some flour in the pan and stir well to combine.

Whisk in the chicken broth and cook on low for 3 minutes. Stir in the half and half and cook for 10 minutes, until thick.

Turn off the heat and mix in the green beans and ¼ of the baked onions. Toss well to combine. Top with the rest of the onions.

Bake for about 10 minutes or until bubbly.

Honey Garlic Roasted Carrots

Ingredients:

2 pounds of thin carrots peeled, tops chopped off or to 2 inches

¼ cup apricot preserves

2 tablespoons olive oil

2 tablespoons honey

1 tablespoon butter, melted

1 teaspoon garlic powder

1 teaspoon balsamic vinegar

¾ teaspoon salt

¼ teaspoon dried thyme leaves

¼ teaspoon dry ground mustard

⅛ teaspoon ground cumin

⅛ teaspoon pepper

Preparation:

Preheat your oven to 375 degrees.

Spray a baking sheet with non-stick spray and place the carrots in the center.

Combine all the remaining ingredients in a bowl, then pour over the carrots. Mix well and spread out in a single layer.

Bake for about 30 minutes until crisp tender.

Roast for longer, if desired. Serve hot and garnish with parsley.

Scalloped Potatoes

Ingredients:

3 pounds of russet potatoes, cut in half lengthwise and sliced thin

3½ cups sharp cheddar cheese, shredded

4 cups milk

1 cup panko bread crumbs

⅓ cup flour

⅓ cup butter

1 teaspoon salt

½ teaspoon onion powder

salt and pepper, to taste

Preparation:

Preheat your oven to 400 degrees.

Lightly grease a 9x13 baking dish and arrange half of the potatoes in the dish, in a single layer. Sprinkle with pepper and salt.

Melt the butter in a saucepan over medium heat and stir in

onion powder, flour and salt. Cook for 1 minute.

Stir in the milk and bring to a gentle boil, then lower the heat to simmer for 10 minutes.

Add in all the cheeses and stir until melted.

Pour half the cheese mixture over the potatoes in the baking dish and arrange the remaining potatoes in a single layer. Season with pepper and salt and finish off with the cheese mix.

Sprinkle with Panko, cover with foil and bake for 1½ hours.

Let rest 20 minutes before serving.

Millionaire Cranberry Salad

Ingredients:

3 cups fresh cranberries

2 cups flaked coconut

2 cups mini marshmallows

2 cups pineapple tidbits, well drained

2 cups sour cream (or plain Greek yogurt)

1 cup chopped pecans

1 cup water

¾ cup sugar

1 cinnamon Stick

Preparation:

Mix the cranberries, cinnamon stick, water and sugar in a saucepan over medium heat and bring to a boil. Lower the heat and simmer for 10 minutes. Remove from heat and allow to cool completely.

Combine 1½ cups of the cooled mixture with the remaining ingredients. Stir well then let stand overnight for the best results or at least 4 hours.

Mac & Cheese Bites

Ingredients:

½ pound macaroni

2 cups sharp cheddar cheese, shredded

1½ cups milk

1 egg beaten

2 ounces of cream cheese

2 tablespoons flour

2 tablespoons butter

½ teaspoon salt

¼ teaspoon pepper

Preparation:

Preheat your oven to 400 degrees.

Coat your mini muffin tins with non-stick cooking spray.

Prepare the pasta according to package instructions then set aside.

Prepare a roux by combining the butter and flour in a skillet over medium heat. Add the milk and stir until smooth. Stir in cream cheese, 1½ cups of cheese, pepper and salt and cook until nice and creamy. Turn off the heat.

Combine the pasta, egg, and cheese sauce in a large bowl and toss well to combine. Spoon the mac and cheese into the muffin tins and bake for 15 minutes. Let stand for 5 minutes before serving.

Creamed Spinach

Ingredients:

2 (10 ounce) packages frozen chopped spinach, thawed and well drained (or use fresh equivalent)

1 cup heavy cream

4 ounces of cream cheese

½ cup parmesan cheese, grated

3 tablespoons butter

1 teaspoon onion powder

2 cloves garlic, minced

1 tablespoon butter

salt and pepper

Preparation:

Add 3 tablespoons of butter to a skillet over medium heat and sauté the onion powder and garlic.

Add the spinach and lower the heat to cook until wilted, for 5 minutes.

In a different pot combine the cream cheese with 1 tablespoon of butter, parmesan and heavy cream. Cook until melted. Season with pepper and salt and whisk well to combine.

Pour the cheesy sauce over the spinach.

Serve immediately.

Garlic Ranch Mashed Potatoes

Ingredients:

4 pounds red potatoes

1 cup of sour cream or Greek yogurt

4 tablespoons butter

⅔ cup quality ranch dressing

4 cloves fresh garlic

milk or cream

salt & pepper to taste

Preparation:

Clean the potatoes and cut into large chunks. Peel and cut garlic into three slices per clove.

Boil garlic together with the potatoes in a pot of salted water for 15 minutes, until soft.

Drain and mash the garlic and potatoes. Add in the remaining ingredients and continue mashing to desired consistency. Add some milk to make them softer, if needed.

Serve warm.

Roasted Root Vegetables

Ingredients:

2 parsnips

2 carrots

1 butternut squash

1 red onion

1 large beet

1 celery root

1 tablespoon apple cider vinegar (more or less to taste)

⅓ cup olive oil

juice from 1 lemon

1 teaspoon dry mustard

¼ cup raw pecans (or walnuts)

sea salt & fresh ground black pepper to taste

parsley leaves, chopped

Preparation:

Preheat your oven to 425 degrees.

Chop the veggies into small chunks and toss with sea salt and oil.

Roast for about 40 minutes until soft.

Toast the pecans in a skillet. Set aside to cool, then chop coarsely.

Whisk the lemon juice, vinegar and mustard in a bowl. Season with pepper and salt and drizzle over the vegetables. Add in the nuts and toss well.

Apple Sausage & Cranberry Stuffing

Ingredients:

5½ cups sourdough bread (or French baguette), cubed & dried

2½ cups whole grain wheat bread, cubed & dried

1¼ cups dried cranberries

2-3 large carrots, chopped

1¼ cups celery, chopped

1½ cups yellow onion, chopped

1 large Granny Smith apple, cored & coarsely chopped

1 large Golden Delicious apple, cored & coarsely chopped

1½ pounds ground pork sausage

3 tablespoons fresh sage leaves, chopped

2 tablespoons fresh rosemary leaves, chopped

2½ teaspoons fresh thyme leaves, chopped

¾ cup Golden Tangerine Turkey Giblet Stock (or turkey stock)

¾ cup quality dry white wine (such as Sauvignon Blanc)

½ cup fresh parsley, finely chopped

6 tablespoons unsalted butter, melted

Preparation:

Preheat your oven to 350 degrees.

Prepare two baking sheets by lining them with parchment paper.

Arrange the sourdough/baguette and whole wheat bread cubes on the sheets and bake for about 10 minutes until golden, tossing half way through the cook time. Remove from oven and transfer the bread cubes to a large bowl to cool.

Cook the onion and sausage in a large skillet over medium heat, until well browned. Chop any large chunks with a spatula. Add the carrots, herbs and celery and cook until soft, for 2 minutes.

Pour the sausage over the bread cubes and toss well to combine. Add the cranberries, apples and parsley and toss once again.

Drizzle the melted butter, wine and stock over the mixture and mix well, until evenly coated. Set aside to cool completely.

Slowly spoon the stuffing into your turkey's cavity.

If you want to bake the stuffing on its own, bake in a well-greased casserole dish and bake for about 40 minutes, covered. Remove from oven and add two tablespoons of butter on top then bake for 10 minutes, until crisp.

Best Ever Dinner Rolls

Ingredients:

6 cups all-purpose flour

2 large eggs

2 cups warm milk

6 tablespoons salted butter, softened

¼ cup white granulated sugar

2 tablespoons instant dry yeast

2 teaspoons salt

1 tablespoon melted butter

Preparation:

Add warm milk, butter, yeast, eggs, sugar and salt in the bowl of a stand mixer.

Mix in 5½ cups of flour and use the dough hook to work the dough on medium speed. Gradually, add the remaining flour and continue mixing until you get a soft and slightly sticky dough and it pulls from the sides of the bowl.

Transfer the dough to a greased bowl and cover with a kitchen towel for 90 minutes.

Grease a baking sheet and make 24 rolls from the dough. Arrange on the baking sheet, cover and let rise for 60 minutes. Preheat your oven to 375 degrees, 30 minutes into the rest time for the rolls.

Bake for about 12 minutes until they turn golden.

Remove from oven and brush with the melted butter and serve warm.

Cheddar Biscuits

Ingredients:

2 cups all-purpose flour

1½ cups sharp cheddar cheese, shredded

1 cup buttermilk

½ cup unsalted butter, melted

1 tablespoon baking powder

1 tablespoon sugar

2 teaspoons garlic powder

½ teaspoon kosher salt

¼ teaspoon cayenne pepper

Topping Ingredients:

3 tablespoons unsalted butter, melted

½ teaspoon garlic powder

1 tablespoon fresh parsley leaves, chopped

Preparation:

Preheat your oven to 450 degrees.

Line a baking sheet with a silicone baking mat or parchment paper, then set aside.

Mix the flour, baking powder, cayenne pepper, garlic powder, sugar and salt in a large bowl.

In a separate bowl, combine the butter and buttermilk. Pour over the bowl of dry ingredients and stir well, until moist. Fold in the cheese using a rubber spatula.

Use a ¼ cup measuring cup and scoop the dough onto the baking sheet and bake for about 10 minutes until golden.

Meanwhile, combine the butter, garlic powder and parsley and brush over the biscuits.

Serve hot.

Herb Roasted Mushrooms

Ingredients:

2 pounds of cremini mushrooms

¼ cup butter

2 cloves garlic, chopped

1 tablespoon lemon juice

1 tablespoon oil

1 teaspoon thyme, chopped

salt and pepper to taste

Preparation:

Preheat your oven to 400 degrees.

Combine the oil, pepper and salt in a bowl, then add in the mushrooms until evenly coated.

Arrange on a baking sheet in one layer and roast for 20 minutes or until they start browning, turning halfway through cook time.

Meanwhile, add the butter to a skillet on medium heat until it starts browning and smelling nutty. Turn off the heat and stir in the lemon juice, thyme and garlic.

Add the roasted mushrooms to the skillet and toss until evenly coated. Adjust seasoning, if desired. Serve hot.

Potatoes Au Gratin

Ingredients:

7 small potatoes

1½ cups sharp white cheddar cheese, shredded

1½ cups heavy cream

2 tablespoons butter, softened

½ cup whole milk

2 tablespoons all-purpose flour

4 cloves of garlic, minced

1 teaspoon salt

pepper

fresh chives, thinly sliced

Preparation:

Preheat your oven to 400 degrees.

Grease a shallow baking dish, then set aside.

Cut the potatoes into cubes and arrange them in the prepared dish.

Mix the cream and milk in a bowl. Stir in the garlic, flour, pepper and salt until well combined and pour over the potatoes.

Cover the dish with foil and bake for half an hour.

Remove the foil and continue baking for about 20 minutes. Sprinkle with the cheese and bake for 5 more minutes, until bubbly.

Garnish with the chives and serve.

Sweet Potato Casserole

Ingredients:

3 pounds of sweet potatoes, peeled & chopped into large chunks

¼ cup half and half

2 tablespoons brown sugar, packed

2 tablespoons unsalted butter

½ teaspoon ground cinnamon (or pumpkin pie spice)

salt to taste

Topping Ingredients:

3 cups mini marshmallows

½ cup chopped pecans

4 tablespoons unsalted butter, softened

¼ cup all-purpose flour

¼ cup brown sugar

½ teaspoon ground cinnamon

⅛ teaspoon salt

Preparation:

Preheat your oven to 375 degrees.

Grease a large casserole dish, then set aside.

Cook the sweet potatoes in a large pot of water until soft. Drain the sweet potatoes, leaving them in the pot. Add milk, butter, brown sugar, cinnamon and salt to the pot and mash the potatoes until creamy. Adjust seasonings, if needed.

Scoop the mashed sweet potatoes into the casserole dish and bake for about 3-5 minutes until heated through.

Meanwhile, combine the brown sugar, butter, pecans, cinnamon, salt and flour, until well combined.

Remove the casserole from the oven and top with about half of the marshmallows. Sprinkle with the prepared pecan topping. Finish off with the remaining marshmallows.

Return to the oven and bake for about 10 minutes, until bubbly and the marshmallows are slightly browned.

Serve hot.

Desserts

Gingerbread Cupcakes

Ingredients:

1½ cups all-purpose flour

1½ cups butter

1 cup sugar

½ cup brown sugar

4 eggs, room temperature

3 tablespoons molasses

2 tablespoons ground ginger

2 teaspoons cinnamon

1½ teaspoons vanilla

¼ teaspoon nutmeg

¼ teaspoon ground cloves

Frosting Ingredients:

4 ounces of cream cheese, softened

4 cups powdered sugar

3 tablespoons heavy cream

1 tablespoon cinnamon

½ teaspoon vanilla

Preparation:

Preheat oven to 350 degrees.

Line muffin tins using cupcake liners and set aside.

In a bowl, whisk together flour, cloves, nutmeg, cinnamon and ginger. Set aside.

In a separate bowl, beat together sugar and butter until light and fluffy. Beat in molasses until well blended. Beat in the eggs, one at a time, until well combined. Beat in vanilla and gently mix in the flour mixture until well blended.

Evenly divide the batter among the cups, filling up to ¾ full; bake for about 25 minutes or until a toothpick inserted in the center comes out clean.

Remove from oven and let cool in muffin tins for at least 10 minutes, and then transfer to wire racks. Let cool completely.

Make the frosting: in a bowl, beat cream cheese for about 2 minutes or until fluffy. Beat in 2 tablespoons of heavy cream, vanilla and cinnamon until smooth. Gradually, beat in powdered sugar. Beat in 1-2 tablespoon of heavy cream or as much is needed to thin out the frosting.

Spread the frosting over cupcakes and enjoy! Store the cupcakes in an airtight container.

Pumpkin Pie

Ingredients:

9" pie crust, unbaked

1 (15 ounce) can pumpkin puree

1 cup brown sugar, packed

3 eggs

½ cup evaporated milk

½ cup heavy whipping cream

2 teaspoons pumpkin pie spice

¼ teaspoon salt

Garnish: whipped topping

Preparation:

Preheat oven to 400 degrees.

Roll out the pie crust and press it into a 9-inch pie pan.

In a large bowl, combine the ingredients, except eggs. Mix until well blended. Whisk in the eggs, one at a time, until the mixture is light and fluffy. Pour into the pie crust.

Bake for about 10 minutes. Lower heat to 350 degrees and bake for 35-40 minutes more.

Remove from oven and cool.

Refrigerate covered, until ready to serve.

Sweet Potato Pie

Crust Ingredients:

2 cups raw pecan halves

2 tablespoons agave nectar

2 tablespoons melted coconut oil

¼ teaspoon salt

¼ teaspoon cinnamon

Filling Ingredients:

2 large sweet potatoes

3 eggs, room temperature

1 cup brown sugar, not packed

1 cup evaporated skim milk

1 teaspoon cinnamon

¼ teaspoon salt

¼ teaspoon nutmeg

dash of ginger

dash of allspice

Preparation:

Peel sweet potatoes and dice them into small chunks. Add the potato chunks to a large pot with water and boil for about 30 minutes or until tender. Drain and mash until smooth. Cover with plastic wrap to keep warm.

Chop nuts in a food processor or blender until fine. Stir in the remaining crust ingredients until well blended.

Press the nut mixture into a 9-inch pie pan and refrigerate for about 15 minutes or more, if needed

Bake the crust at 350 degrees for about 10 minutes, or until nuts are toasted.

Meanwhile, beat the mashed potatoes with a mixer until smooth. Beat the remaining filling ingredients until creamy and very smooth.

Remove the crust from the oven and increase oven temperature to 400 degrees. Pour the filling mixture into crust.

Continue baking for about 45 minutes or until the top is slightly browned.

Remove the pie from oven and let cool completely on wire rack.

Christmas Crinkle Cookies

Ingredients:

1 box white cake mix

2 eggs

⅓ cup powdered sugar

⅓ cup canola or vegetable oil

red and green food coloring

Preparation:

Preheat oven to 375 degrees.

In a large bowl, mix together cake mix, oil and eggs. Separate the dough into two equal parts.

In two small bowls, dye one part green and the other red.

Refrigerate the dough for at least 30 minutes to make fluffier cookies.

Roll tablespoon-sized balls of the dough in powdered sugar and arrange them on a parchment paper lined cookie sheet.

Bake for about 9-11 minutes.

Remove from oven and let cool slightly on the cookie sheet.

Transfer to a wire rack and let cool completely.

Gingerbread Fudge

Ingredients:

12 ounces of white chocolate, melted (you can use white chocolate chips)

1 cup sweetened condensed milk

1 teaspoon ground nutmeg

1 teaspoon ground ginger

1 teaspoon ground cinnamon

½ tablespoon green nonpareils (tiny ball sprinkles)

½ tablespoon red nonpareils (tiny ball sprinkles)

Preparation:

In a large bowl, combine sweetened condensed milk and melted white chocolate. Add ginger, cinnamon, and nutmeg. Stir until well combined. Stir in most of the nonpareils, leaving some for the top.

With a spatula, transfer the fudge into a parchment paper lined glass baking dish.

Smoothen the top and sprinkle with the remaining nonpareils. Let sit for a few minutes or until firm.

Cut into squares and serve.

Grinch Crinkle Cookies

You Will Need:

parchment paper

pastry bag

Ingredients:

1 box vanilla cake mix

2 eggs, room temperature

1 stick unsalted butter, softened

1 cup corn starch

1 cup powdered sugar

1 tablespoon canola oil

green gel food coloring

Icing Ingredients:

1 cup powdered sugar

2 egg whites

½ teaspoon cream of tartar

red gel food coloring

Preparation:

Preheat oven to 375 degrees.

Line cookie sheet with parchment paper.

In a loaf pan, combine corn starch and powdered sugar. Mix well.

In a bowl, whisk together eggs, oil, butter and cake mix to form a thick batter. Stir in the green food coloring.

With an ice cream scoop, scoop out dough and then roll into sugar mixture. Roll dough into a ball. Arrange the balls onto a cookie sheet.

Bake for about 8-10 minutes or until puffed up.

Remove from oven and let cool slightly on the cookie sheet. Transfer to a wire rack and let cool completely.

Gingerbread Bread Pudding

Ingredients:

1 loaf Texas Toast, cut into 1" cubes

5 eggs

2½ cups milk

⅔ cup brown sugar, packed

¼ cup molasses

1½ teaspoon cinnamon

1 teaspoon vanilla

1 teaspoon ginger

½ teaspoon allspice

½ teaspoon nutmeg

Vanilla Sauce Ingredients:

1 (14 ounce) can sweetened condensed milk

1 ½ cup sugar

1 ½ stick unsalted butter, slightly melted

2 teaspoons vanilla

1 egg yolk

Preparation:

Preheat oven to 350 degrees.

Place the bread on the baking sheet and bake, stirring halfway through, for about 10 minutes or until crisp.

Take bread out of the oven and place into a large bowl.

In a separate bowl, whisk together milk, molasses, vanilla, eggs, spices and sugar until combined.

Pour the mixture over the bread and stir until well absorbed. Let sit for 10-15 minutes.

In the meantime, grease a 2-quart baking pan with non-stick cooking spray. Spoon the bread mixture into the pan.

Bake for about 45-60 minutes, or until the center is set. Remove from oven and let cool slightly.

Make the sauce: in a saucepan, combine butter and sugar. Stir until well mixed. Cook over medium-high heat until butter is melted and the mixture is creamy.

In a large bowl, beat the egg. Gradually, whisk in the sauce and stir in vanilla.

Pour the sauce over the bread pudding and enjoy!

Snowman Cupcakes

Ingredients:

premade chocolate cupcakes

vanilla frosting

mini chocolate chips

butterscotch chips

white crystallized decorating sugar

Preparation:

Generously spread frosting over the cupcakes.

Add white crystallized decorating sugar to a small bowl.

Hold the bottom of a cupcake and gently press it down into the sugar, rocking it back and forth in all directions until well covered with sugar. Press hard for the sugar to stick on the icing and the lines created from the icing are smoothed out.

Gently press a regular-sized butterscotch chip into the center of the cupcake for the nose. Decorate with mini chocolate chips for the mouth and eyes.

Black Forest Trifle

Ingredients:

1 box devil's food cake, prepared according to package

1 box of instant chocolate pudding, prepared according to package

1 (21 ounce) can cherry filling

1 tub whipped topping

Preparation:

Crumble the cake into small pieces.

Layer the cake pieces, then cherry filling, then pudding, and lastly, the whipped cream.

Repeat the layers until all ingredients are used up.

Place in the fridge for at least 1 hour. Serve chilled.

Christmas Layer Cake

Shortbread Cookie Layer Ingredients:

1½ cups all-purpose flour

¾ cup unsalted butter, softened

½ cup powdered sugar

1 tablespoon cocoa powder

¼ teaspoon salt

red food coloring

Peppermint Cheesecake Layer Ingredients:

1½ cup whipped topping

8 ounces of cream cheese, softened

1 cup powdered sugar

1 teaspoon peppermint extract

Pudding Layer Ingredients:

2 boxes white chocolate instant pudding

3 cups milk

green food coloring

Topping:

1½ cups whipped topping

Garnishes: 2 cups mini marshmallows, red and green sprinkles, M&M's

Preparation:

Preheat oven to 350 degrees.

Lightly coat a 9×13-inch baking dish with butter and set aside.

In a bowl, mix cocoa powder, flour, and salt.

In another bowl, cream butter and sugar until smooth. Mix in 1 tablespoon of red food coloring. Turn the mixer on low speed and slowly beat in the flour mixture until well blended.

Press the batter into the baking dish.

Bake for about 18-20 minutes. Remove from oven and let cool completely.

Make cream cheese layer by beating powdered sugar and cream cheese until very smooth. Mix in peppermint extract and 1½ cups of whipped topping. Spread the mixture over the shortbread layer and freeze until firm.

Meanwhile, prepare pudding: whisk together 3 cups of milk and 2 boxes of white chocolate instant pudding mix. Whisk in a few drops of green food coloring until smooth.

Spread the pudding over the cream cheese layer and freeze for about 5 minutes.

Spread 1½ cups of whipped topping over the pudding layer. Top with marshmallows and sprinkles.

Refrigerate for about 3-4 hours or until set.

Candy Cane Cupcakes

Ingredients:

1½ cups sugar

2½ cup flour

1 cup sour cream

¾ cup butter, softened

½ cup milk

3 eggs

2 teaspoons baking powder

1 teaspoon vanilla

½ teaspoon baking soda

½ teaspoon salt

¼ cup sprinkles

Buttercream Frosting Ingredients:

3 cups icing sugar

1 cup butter, softened

4 tablespoons whipping cream

2 teaspoon peppermint extract

4 candy canes crushed for topping

Preparation:

Preheat oven to 350 degrees.

Line 24 muffin tins with cupcake liners and set aside.

In a bowl, cream together sugar and butter until fluffy. Beat in eggs, one at a time, until well blended. Beat in milk, sour cream and vanilla. Mix well.

In a separate bowl, whisk together flour, salt, baking soda and baking powder. Gradually, beat the flour into the butter mixture until well blended.

Fold in sprinkles and spoon the batter into prepared muffin tins, ⅔ full.

Bake for about 18-20 minutes or until the cupcakes bounce back when touched. Cool completely on wire racks.

Make icing: in a large bowl, cream butter. Beat in the remaining ingredients until light and fluffy.

Transfer the icing into a piping bad and decorate the cupcakes as desired. Sprinkle with candy canes and keep in covered container until ready to eat.

Refrigerate and remove from the refrigerator 30 minutes before serving.

Bailey's Chocolate Mousse

Ingredients:

½ cup Bailey's Irish Cream, chilled

1½ cup heavy cream, chilled

½ cup sugar

¼ cup boiling water

3 tablespoons cocoa powder

2 tablespoons cold water

2 teaspoons unflavored gelatin

1 teaspoon vanilla

Preparation:

Before starting, freeze the bowl and beaters for at least 15-20 minutes.

In a small bowl, stir cold water and gelatin for about 1 minute or until gelatin softens.

Stir in hot water to dissolve gelatin and let sit to cool.

In a chilled bowl, mix sugar and cocoa and beat in heavy cream until smooth. Slowly beat in gelatin mixture, vanilla and Bailey's until soft peaks form.

Set aside for about 5 minutes to thicken.

Spoon the mixture into dishes and chill for about 1 hour before serving.

Mini Eggnog Cheesecakes

Ingredients:

1 cup graham cracker crumbs

12 ounces of cream cheese, softened

1 egg

2 tablespoons butter, melted

½ cup eggnog

½ cup sugar

1 tablespoon flour

½ teaspoon nutmeg

½ teaspoon vanilla

Preparation:

Preheat oven to 350 degrees.

Line 9 cups of muffin pan with paper liners.

In a bowl, mix together butter, graham cracker crumbs, and ¼ teaspoon nutmeg, until well combined.

Divide the mixture between the prepared muffin cups, pressing to flatten.

In a food processor or with a mixer, blend together sugar and cream cheese until creamy and smooth. Beat in the eggnog, egg, flour, vanilla and ¼ teaspoon nutmeg.

Divide the mixture among the muffin cups until three-quarter full.

Bake for about 20 minutes or until the centers are set. Remove from oven and let cool completely in the pan.

Remove the cakes from the pan and chill in the fridge for a few hours before serving.

Top the cakes with whipped cream and dust with the remaining nutmeg. Enjoy!

Carrot Cake

Ingredients:

3¼ cups all-purpose flour

1 pound fresh carrots, finely grated

1½ cups plus 2 tablespoons vegetable oil

1 cup brown sugar, packed

1 cup granulated sugar

6 eggs

1 tablespoon ground cinnamon

1 tablespoon vanilla extract

2 teaspoons salt

2 teaspoons baking soda

1 teaspoon baking powder

½ teaspoon ground nutmeg

pinch of ground cloves

Optional: 1 cup pecans or walnuts, chopped and ½ cup raisins

Frosting Ingredients:

6 cups powdered sugar, plus extra if needed

3 (8 ounce) packages cream cheese, softened

1 tablespoon vanilla extract

2 sticks unsalted butter, softened

½ teaspoon salt

Preparation:

Preheat oven to 350 degrees.

Grease and lightly flour 3 (8-inch) baking pans.

In a large bowl with a stand mixer, beat together brown sugar, granulated sugar, and oil until very smooth. Beat in eggs, one at a time, until well blended. Beat in vanilla.

In another bowl, whisk together flour, cloves, nutmeg, baking powder, baking soda, cinnamon and salt, until well mixed.

In the bowl of a large stand mixer, mix together oil, granulated sugar, and brown sugar until combined and smooth. Add in the eggs one at a time, then the vanilla, and mix until smooth.

Add to the wet ingredients and beat until well blended. Fold in grated carrots and nuts and/or raisins, if desired.

Divide the batter among the pans and bake for about 25-30 minutes or until a tester inserted in the center comes out clean.

Remove from oven and let cool in the pans for a few minutes before transferring to a wire rack to cool completely.

To make the frosting: in a large bowl with a mixer, beat together all frosting ingredients.

Layer cakes with cream cheese frosting and serve or cover and store for up to four days.

Gingerbread Cheesecake Dip

Ingredients:

8 ounces of cream cheese, softened

½ tub whipped topping

¼ cup powdered sugar, sifted

¼ cup brown sugar

3 tablespoons molasses

1 teaspoon ground cinnamon

1 teaspoon ground ginger

dash nutmeg

graham crackers for serving

Preparation:

With a stand mixer or hand mixer, beat cream cheese for about 1 minute or until smooth. Beat in molasses and sugars for about 1 minute more, or until very smooth and well blended.

Beat in cinnamon, ginger and nutmeg until well combined. Beat in whipped topping for about 30 seconds and transfer the dip to a bowl.

Refrigerate until ready to serve.

Serve dip with graham crackers. You can refrigerate the dip in an air-tight container for up to 7 days.

Eggnog Fudge

Ingredients:

1 (7 ounce) jar marshmallow creme

2 cups white chocolate chips

2 cups sugar

¾ cup eggnog

½ cup butter

2 teaspoons vanilla extract

½ teaspoon nutmeg

Preparation:

Prepare a 9x9-inch pan by lining it with foil. Spray foil with non-stick cooking spray.

In a saucepan, mix eggnog, sugar, and butter. Bring the mixture to a boil. Continue cooking until the temperature reaches 234 degrees.

Remove from heat and stir in white chocolate until melted. Stir in nutmeg, vanilla, and marshmallow crème.

Spread the mixture into the pan and garnish with more nutmeg to serve.

Chocolate Hazelnut Truffles

Filling Ingredients:

3 cups toasted hazelnuts, finely chopped

3 cups hazelnut wafer cookies, crushed

1¼ cup Nutella

Coating Ingredients:

1½ cups toasted hazelnuts, finely chopped

1 cup semisweet chocolate chips

1 teaspoon coconut oil (or vegetable oil)

Preparation:

Start with the filling: prepare a baking sheet by lining it with parchment paper.

In a bowl, crush the hazelnut wafer cookies. Add Nutella and mix well. Refrigerate for about 30 minutes, or until mixture is firm.

Scoop out teaspoon-sized portions and shape into balls. Arrange them on the prepared baking sheet. Freeze for about 15 minutes.

Meanwhile, in a medium bowl, stir together oil and chocolate.

Microwave until chocolate is melted. Stir in hazelnuts until well combined.

Insert toothpicks into the truffles (balls) and dip them into the chocolate mixture. Arrange them onto the baking sheet and refrigerate for about 15 minutes.

Serve the truffles in mini cupcake liners. Enjoy!

White Truffle Cake

Cake Ingredients:

⅓ cup all-purpose flour

⅓ cup sugar

3 eggs

1 teaspoon vanilla extract

Topping Ingredients:

12 ounces of white chocolate chips (or chopped white chocolate)

8 ounces of cream cheese (or mascarpone)

1¼ cup heavy cream

Preparation:

For the Cake Layer:

Preheat oven to 350 degrees.

Grease an 8-inch round spring form pan with butter and dust with flour. Set aside.

In a bowl, beat together sugar, eggs, and vanilla for about 3 minutes, or until foamy. In three batches, fold in flour.

Transfer the batter to the prepared pan.

Bake for about 15-17 minutes or until a tester comes out clean.

Cool the cake completely on wire rack.

For Truffle Topping:

Add cream to a saucepan and bring to a boil. Stir in chopped white chocolate until it melts. Cool the mixture completely.

With a hand mixer, whip in cream cheese or mascarpone until very smooth. Pour the mixture over the cake in the pan and refrigerate for at least 2 hours.

Release the cake from the pan by running a knife along the sides of the pan. Carefully unmold the cake and place it on the cake stand.

Strawberry Chocolate Cake

Cake Ingredients:

1 cup sugar

½ cup boiling water

½ cup milk

1 egg

¾ cup + 2 tablespoons all-purpose flour

¼ cup + 2 tablespoons cocoa

¾ teaspoon baking soda

¾ teaspoon baking powder

½ teaspoon salt

¼ cup vegetable oil

1 teaspoon vanilla extract

Chocolate Mousse Ingredients:

2 quarts of strawberries (the smaller the better)

1 ¾ cups heavy whipping cream

12 ounces of semisweet chocolate, chopped (or chips)

3.5 ounces of white chocolate, chopped (or chips)

⅔ cup powdered sugar

6 tablespoons unsalted butter

2½ tablespoons cool water

2 teaspoons unflavored gelatin

1½ teaspoons vanilla extract

Chocolate Ganache Ingredients:

5.5 ounces of semisweet chocolate, chopped (or chips)

⅔ cup heavy whipping cream

Chocolate Curl Ingredients:

3.5 ounces semisweet baking chocolate

1 tablespoon vegetable shortening (or vegetable oil)

Preparation:

Make the Cake:

Preheat oven to 350 degrees.

Grease a 9-inch baking pan with butter and line the bottom with parchment paper.

In a large bowl, mix the dry ingredients. Beat in the oil, milk, egg, and vanilla, until well combined. Add half a cup of water and beat until well blended.

Transfer batter to a pan and bake for about 25-35 minutes, or until a tester comes out clean.

Remove from oven and let cool for about 10 minutes in the pan.

Transfer to wire racks to cool completely.

Make the Chocolate Mousse Filling:

Soften 2 teaspoons of unflavored gelatin is a small dish with 2½ tablespoons cold water. Set aside.

Mix butter, white chocolate and chopped semi-sweet chocolate in a heat-proof bowl. Microwave until chocolate is melted, stirring between 30 second intervals.

On low heat, cook the softened gelatin, stirring, until dissolved. Set aside to cool.

In a bowl, combine vanilla and heavy cream until well mixed. Gradually, beat in powdered sugar and then mix in gelatin.

Whisk a few tablespoons of whipped cream into the butter-chocolate mixture until lightened. Add the mixture into the remaining whipped cream and stir with a spatula until well incorporated.

Assemble the Cake:

put the cake onto a plate, and set the ring from a springform pan around the cake.

Spread the cake with a thin layer of the chocolate mousse filling.

Remove stems from the strawberries and vertically cut some into halves.

Arrange the strawberry halves around the edges of the pan and then fill the entire bottom with whole strawberries.

Fill a piping bag with the filling and fill all gaps that are between strawberries.

Spread the remaining mousse over the strawberries and smoothen the top. Refrigerate for about 4-6 hours to set.

Make Ganache:

In a saucepan, simmer 2/3 cup heavy cream. Pour over 5½ ounces chopped chocolate and let sit for a few minutes, stirring, until chocolate melts.

Spread the ganache over the cake and return back to the fridge for a few minutes or until ganache is set.

Run a knife around your cake to release the ring from the pan.

Make Chocolate Curls:

In a saucepan, heat 1 tablespoon of vegetable shortening and 3½ ounces semisweet chocolate until chocolate is melted.

Spread a thin layer of the chocolate mixture onto the baking sheet and freeze for about 6-8 minutes or until firm.

Remove from the freezer and let sit for about 2 minutes. Scrape along the edges of the chocolate with a metal spatula to make the curls.

Arrange the chocolate curls over the cake and garnish with more strawberries.

Store the cake in the fridge.

Red Velvet Ice Cream Cake

Cheesecake Ice Cream Ingredients:

1 (14 ounce) can sweetened condensed milk

2 cups heavy whipping cream

4 ounces of cream cheese, softened

Cake Ingredients:

2¼ cups all-purpose flour

1½ cups sugar

1 cup buttermilk

½ cup butter, softened

2 large eggs

2 tablespoons cocoa powder

1 teaspoon salt

3 tablespoons red food coloring

1 teaspoon distilled white vinegar

1 teaspoon vanilla extract

1 teaspoon baking soda

Frosting Ingredients:

2 cups heavy whipping cream

½ cup powdered sugar

Preparation:

Beat together sweetened condensed milk and cream cheese in a large bowl.

In another bowl, beat cream until stiff peaks form. Fold the cream into the milk mixture.

Line two (9-inch) baking pans with plastic wrap and divide the cream mixture equally between the two pans. Smoothen the tops.

Freeze, covered with plastic wrap, for at least 6 hours or until solid.

Make Cake Layers:

preheat oven to 350 degrees.

Line three (9-inch) cake pans with parchment paper. Coat with non-stick cooking spray.

In a bowl, combine flour, salt and cocoa powder.

In a separate bowl with a mixer, beat together sugar and butter for about 5 minutes or until very smooth. Whisk in the eggs until well combined.

Beat in one-third of the flour mixture, then half of buttermilk, followed by another one-third of the flour mixture.

Beat in the remaining buttermilk and flour mixture, beating well after every addition. Whisk in vanilla and red food coloring.

In small bowl, mix baking soda and vinegar. Fold into the batter and divide the mixture equally among the three cake pans.

Bake for about 20 minutes or until cake springs back when touched.

Remove the cakes from oven and let cool for about 10 minutes in pans, and then transfer to wire rack to cool completely.

Make the Frosting and Assemble:

In large bowl, beat cream until stiff peaks form. Gradually, beat in powdered sugar until smooth,

Level the cake layer, if needed. Place a cake layer on a cake plate or cake stand.

Add one layer of ice cream over the cake and add another cake layer. Then add another ice cream layer, and top with the last cake layer.

· Frost with whipped cream and decorate, if desired. Freeze until ready to use.

Sugar Cookie Truffles

Ingredients:

12 premade sugar cookies

2 cups white chocolate chips

3 tablespoons cream cheese, softened

Sprinkles

Preparation:

In a food processor, process the sugar cookies into fine crumbs. Add the cream cheese and continue processing until well blended. Shape the batter into 1-inch balls.

Arrange the balls onto a cookie sheet lined with parchment paper and refrigerate for about 1 hour.

In a bowl, melt the chocolate, in the microwave. Microwave for 30 second intervals until melted, stirring between each interval.

Remove the balls from the fridge and with a fork, dip them, one at a time, into chocolate until well coated.

Return them onto the cookie sheet and top with sprinkles.

Store in airtight container in the refrigerator for up to one week.

Thank you for reading my Christmas recipe book! I hope you have as much fun as I do cooking for the holidays. If you have a couple of spare minutes, please leave a helpful review for others!

Made in the USA
Middletown, DE
17 December 2021